Self-Empowerment Secrets Exposed
Volume 1

Ronald Roscoe

i

Dedication

This book is dedicated to Sueboo, you never left me no matter how bad or ugly things got. To my sons, JaVion and Jaylon Roscoe. You are my world and my legacy. This journey and the lessons within are for you, to guide you and anyone who seeks a path toward personal empowerment and lasting success.

Acknowledgments

I want to personally thank GOD for pushing me through this rigorous process of pain and pressure to build this indestructible character within me on self.

Foreword

In life, we all face obstacles. Some are minor, while others seem insurmountable, but within each challenge lies the potential for growth, resilience, and transformation. The TSO Self-Empowerment Secrets Exposed, Volume 1 is a journey of such transformation—one that started in the unforgiving streets of Birmingham, Alabama, and led to a life dedicated to self-empowerment and financial freedom.

Ronald Roscoe, the author and founder of TSO Enterprises Inc., knows this journey firsthand. Raised amidst environments that often limit potential rather than foster it, he faced his share of adversity and hard lessons. But through those experiences, he found a deeper purpose and a calling that transcends his circumstances. His story reflects a powerful truth: No matter where we start, we can choose a path that aligns with our highest vision of ourselves.

This book isn't just a collection of principles; it's a blueprint for taking control of your life, transforming your mindset, and achieving empowerment through both personal growth and financial literacy. Ronald's words come from a place of authenticity and hard-won wisdom, drawn from years of self-reflection and a commitment to change.

Volume 1 lays the groundwork for true self-empowerment, touching on foundational topics such as resilience, financial literacy, and goal-setting. But more than that, it offers practical guidance and actionable steps, ensuring that each reader can begin applying these principles immediately.

Ronald's story is proof that even in the darkest moments, we have the power to rewrite our own narrative. This guide is for anyone ready to embrace that power, to push beyond limitations, and to build a future of prosperity and purpose.

Introduction

The TSO Self-Empowerment Secrets Exposed; Vol. 1 is more than a book; it's a guide to transforming your life. Born out of my own journey through adversity, it seeks to inspire and motivate, laying out fundamental tools to set you on a path to empowerment. Through a mixture of personal stories, practical insights, and actionable steps, this volume explores ways to overcome limiting beliefs and tap into your potential, showing that success is within reach no matter where you start.

The TSO's Self-Empowerment Secrets Exposed, Vol. 1 isn't just a guide, it's the beginning of a transformative journey. As someone who grew up in Birmingham, Alabama, surrounded by hardship, I was raised in a world that taught me survival skills in ways I didn't initially recognize. Influenced by those around me, I learned the rules of the streets, the hustle, and what seemed like my path at the time. My natural charisma and talent on the basketball court gave me early success, but the allure of fast money in the streets drew me in deeper.

Through each stage of life, I encountered choices that would shape me. Moving from Alabama to Las Vegas and back, I spiraled into situations that led to state prison to serve 5 years, where I thought I understood survival. When I was later sent to federal prison, serving 12 years, I finally had the time and motivation to reevaluate everything. Those years weren't just spent behind bars; they were an opportunity to redefine who I was and to understand my true purpose. There, I discovered a passion for economics and financial empowerment, not just for myself but to help others escape the cycles of poverty and hardship.

In this book, I share the lessons learned on my journey, providing tools to empower and inspire. With TSO Enterprises Inc., my mission is to help others navigate the path of self-empowerment, financial independence, and purpose-driven success.

Contents

Chapter 1: The Power of Inspiration and Belief

Every journey toward self-empowerment starts with inspiration. Understanding the power of belief in yourself is essential. Many of us grow up feeling boxed in by the limitations of our environment. In my early years, I found myself caught in cycles that seemed inescapable, but realizing that change possibly became my turning point.

Key Concepts:
1. **Embracing Your Story:**
   - Recognize that every hardship shapes who you are.
2. **Visualizing Success:**
   - Practice envisioning your future success as a daily routine.
3. **Setting Achievable Goals:**
   - Break down goals into actionable, manageable steps.

Actionable Steps:
1. **Reflection Exercise:**
   - Write down three personal strengths. How have these traits helped you overcome challenges?
2. **Visualization Practice:**
   - Spend five minutes each morning visualizing your goals.
3. **Goal Setting:**
   - Start with a single, small goal for the week that aligns with your larger vision.

Chapter 2: Motivation and Purpose

Motivation is the fuel that keeps you moving toward your goals, and understanding your purpose is the anchor that holds you steady. When I was at my lowest, my purpose became my motivation—my family, my dreams, and the desire to change my life. This clarity propelled me forward, even when things got tough.

Key Concepts:
1. **Identifying Your 'Why':**
   - Discover what drives you.
2. **Maintaining Discipline:**
   - Recognize the difference between motivation and discipline.
3. **Avoiding Complacency:**
   - Stay focused on continual growth.

Actionable Steps:
1. **Purpose Reflection:**
   - Write down why each goal is important to you.
2. **Daily Affirmations:**
   - Start each day with affirmations that reinforce your purpose.
3. **Set Milestones:**
   - Break larger goals into achievable, weekly milestones.

Chapter 3: Building Resilience

Resilience is the capacity to recover from setbacks and keep pushing forward. For me, resilience was the key to overcoming every obstacle on my path to personal empowerment. Learning to bounce back taught me that failure is only a detour—not a dead-end.

Key Concepts:
1. **Embracing Failure as a Teacher:**
   - Each setback is a lesson.
2. **Strengthening Your Mindset:**
   - Cultivate mental toughness.
3. **Adaptability:**
   - Flexibility helps you thrive in changing situations.

Actionable Steps:
1. **Self-Reflection:**
   - Analyze past failures and identify lessons.
2. **Positive Self-Talk:**
   - Replace negative thoughts with empowering affirmations.
3. **Challenge Comfort Zones:**
   - Regularly engage in activities that push your limits.

Chapter 4: Developing a Growth Mindset

A growth mindset is the belief that abilities and intelligence can be developed through dedication and hard work. This mentality sets the foundation for resilience and success. Adopting a growth mindset transformed my life; it allowed me to see potential in every challenge.

Key Concepts:
1. **Viewing Challenges as Opportunities**
2. **Embracing Effort as a Path to Mastery**
3. **Learning from Criticism**

Actionable Steps:
1. **Set Learning Goals:**
   - Focus on growth over immediate results.
2. **Practice Persistence:**
   - Keep going, especially when it's hard.
3. **Seek Feedback:**
   - Learn from others to improve continuously.

Chapter 5: Building Self-Discipline

Self-discipline is the cornerstone of lasting change. It empowers you to push through discomfort, delay gratification, and stay focused on your goals. I had to cultivate self-discipline during my journey; it became my shield against distractions.

Key Concepts:
1. **Setting Clear Boundaries**
2. **Building Routines for Consistency**
3. **Developing Willpower**

Actionable Steps:
1. **Set Small, Achievable Goals:**
   - Break down larger goals.
2. **Create a Routine:**
   - Find consistency in daily tasks.
3. **Reward Yourself:**
   - Acknowledge progress to build motivation.

Chapter 6: Harnessing the Power of a Growth Mindset

A growth mindset opens the door to possibilities by embracing challenges and valuing learning over comfort. Developing this mindset during my transformation allowed me to see setbacks as lessons.

Key Concepts:
1. **Belief in Personal Growth**
2. **Viewing Challenges as Opportunities**
3. **Embracing Learning and Adaptability**

Actionable Steps:
1. **Challenge Negative Self-Talk:**
   - Reframe limiting beliefs.
2. **Pursue Learning Opportunities:**
   - Invest in personal growth.
3. **Set Stretch Goals:**
   - Push beyond your comfort zone.

Chapter 7: Building a Resilient Foundation

Resilience means staying committed despite setbacks. In prison, I learned resilience isn't just about surviving but thriving with purpose. With the right foundation, we can achieve anything.

Key Concepts:
1. **Embracing Failure as Feedback**
2. **Finding Strength in Purpose**
3. **Mental Fortitude**

Actionable Steps:
1. **Reflect on Setbacks:**
   - Write lessons learned from challenges.
2. **Develop a Support System:**
   - Surround yourself with those who lift you up.
3. **Practice Self-Care:**
   - Build habits that strengthen your mind and body.

Chapter 8: Embracing Personal Accountability

Accountability means taking responsibility for our actions and choices. I learned that true growth stems from owning my decisions, even the tough ones, and aligning them with my values and goals.

Key Concepts:
1. **Self-Awareness and Ownership**
2. **Building Trust through Transparency**
3. **Commitment to Growth**

Actionable Steps:
1. **Daily Reflection:**
   - Journal to understand your choices and areas for improvement.
2. **Set Personal Standards:**
   - Define the values you'll hold yourself accountable to.
3. **Seek Feedback:**
   - Use constructive feedback as a tool for growth.

Chapter 9: Mastering Financial Literacy

Understanding and controlling finances is foundational to empowerment. Financial literacy means knowing how money works, how to manage it, and how to make it grow. My journey into financial awareness began by acknowledging the importance of knowledge over quick gains.

Key Concepts:

1. **Budgeting**
   - Recognize the importance of a structured budget. This is more than listing expenses; it's a roadmap to financial security.
   - Every dollar should have a purpose—whether it's bills, savings, investments, or personal spending.

2. **Debt Management**
   - Learn to differentiate between "good" and "bad" debt. Good debt, like mortgages or student loans, can build assets, while bad debt, like high-interest credit cards, can be a financial burden.
   - Strategies to reduce debt, like prioritizing high-interest balances, can make a massive difference in financial stability.

3. **Saving & Investing**
   - Saving is the foundation, but investing is how you build wealth. Understanding different investment options (stocks, real estate, bonds) can transform how you think about long-term growth.
     - Compounding interest is a powerful tool, especially in retirement accounts, that can exponentially grow wealth over time.

4. **Understanding Credit Scores**
   - Your credit score is a financial report card. It affects loan approvals, interest rates, and sometimes even job opportunities.

- Building and maintaining good credit is about smart borrowing, on-time payments, and low credit utilization.

5. **Insurance and Risk Management**
   - Protecting assets through insurance can mitigate risks, providing a safety net for unexpected events like accidents or health issues.
   - Knowing the types of insurance (health, life, property) and when to use them helps secure financial well-being.

Actionable Steps:

1. **Create a Monthly Budget:**
   - Write down your income and categorize expenses. Track spending and adjust as needed to ensure you save a portion each month.

2. **Set Debt Reduction Goals:**
   - Start with high-interest debts, then tackle others. Explore debt consolidation options if needed.

3. **Start an Emergency Fund:**
   - Aim to save at least three to six months' worth of expenses for unforeseen circumstances.

4. **Educate Yourself on Investments:**
   - Begin learning about stocks, bonds, and mutual funds. Start small—experience will build confidence.

5. **Check Your Credit Report Regularly:**
   - Monitor your credit for discrepancies and look for ways to improve. Aim for a score that unlocks better financial opportunities.

6. **Explore Insurance Options:**
   - Ensure you're covered with essential insurances that match your needs.

Chapter 10: Building and Maintaining Good Credit

Credit is not only a tool but a key to broader financial opportunities. Early on, I learned that managing credit well could unlock options for investments, business growth, and financial security.

Key Concepts:

1. **Credit Utilization**
   - Credit utilization refers to the ratio of your credit card balances to the credit limits. Keeping utilization low (below 30%) can significantly impact your score positively.

2. **On-Time Payments**
   - Every missed payment can damage your credit score, affecting your credibility with lenders. Consistently paying on time reflects financial responsibility.

3. **Types of Credit Accounts**
   - Lenders favor a mix of credit types—like credit cards, installment loans, and mortgages—as it shows versatility and reliability in handling different types of debt.

4. **Length of Credit History**
   - A longer history with credit accounts boosts your score. Avoid closing old accounts, as their length contributes positively to your credit.

5. **Credit Inquiries**
   - Hard inquiries (e.g., loan applications) can slightly lower your score. Limit applications to avoid unnecessary inquiries that signal potential financial strain.

Actionable Steps:

1. **Monitor Your Credit Regularly:**
   - Checking your report allows you to spot and correct any errors.
2. **Keep Balances Low:**
   - Aim to pay off your balances in full each month to maintain low credit utilization.
3. **Establish Automated Payments:**
   - Set up automatic payments to avoid missed payments and maintain a consistent history.
4. **Limit Hard Inquiries:**
   - Space out loan applications to protect your score from frequent hard pulls.
5. **Open Credit Only When Needed:**
   - Avoid opening unnecessary accounts, which can lower your score initially.

Chapter 11: Financial Literacy Essentials

Understanding financial literacy is foundational to managing and growing your wealth. This knowledge can enable you to make informed decisions, avoid pitfalls, and seize financial opportunities.

Key Concepts:
1. **Budgeting**:
   - A budget is a structured plan that allocates income towards expenses, savings, and investments, serving as a roadmap for spending.
2. **Saving & Investing:**
   - Building a savings habit ensures funds for emergencies. Investing grows your wealth through assets like stocks, bonds, or real estate.
3. **Debt Management:**
   - Distinguishing between good debt (e.g., mortgages, business loans) and bad debt (e.g., high-interest consumer debt) is crucial. Focus on paying down high-interest debts first.
4. **Understanding Interest Rates:**
   - Interest rates affect borrowing costs and investment growth. Learn to identify high and low-interest opportunities to make informed choices.

Actionable Steps:
1. **Create a Budget:**
   - Track income and expenses monthly, adjusting as necessary to meet financial goals.

2. **Establish Emergency Savings:**
   - Aim for three to six months' worth of expenses to buffer against unexpected events.
3. **Set Clear Financial Goals:**
   - Whether for retirement, education, or a home, knowing your goals drives informed financial decisions.
4. **Limit High-Interest Debt:**
   - Prioritize paying off high-interest obligations to free up resources for investments.
5. **Educate Yourself on Investments:**
   - Start small, with assets like ETFs or mutual funds, and gradually expand your portfolio as knowledge grows.

Chapter 12: Building Personal Credit

Credit is crucial for financial opportunities, from buying a home to securing business funding. A strong credit score reflects responsible borrowing and trustworthiness in the eyes of lenders.

Key Concepts:

1. **Credit Scores and Reports:**
   - Understanding credit scores (from 300 to 850) and the elements that affect them (payment history, credit utilization, length of credit history, etc.) is essential.
2. **Credit Utilization:**
   - The percentage of credit you use affects your score. Aim for under 30% usage per card to maintain a positive impact.
3. **Types of Credit:**
   - Diversifying your credit types (e.g., credit cards, installment loans) helps build a robust credit history.

Actionable Steps:

1. **Monitor Your Credit Report:**
   - Review it regularly to check for errors and identify areas to improve.
2. **Make On-Time Payments:**
   - Consistently paying bills on time boosts your credit score significantly.
3. **Limit New Credit Applications:**
   - Frequent credit inquiries can lower your score. Only apply for new credit when necessary.

4. **Pay Down Balances:**
   - Lowering outstanding balances can improve your credit utilization ratio.
5. **Consider Secured Credit Cards:**
   - These cards, backed by a deposit, are helpful for building or rebuilding credit responsibly.

Chapter 13: Building a Financial Network

A strong financial network provides opportunities for career growth, business ventures, and access to knowledge and resources. Connections with like-minded individuals who share similar goals are essential to financial empowerment.

Key Concepts:

1. **Networking:**
   - Networking is about mutual growth and shared learning. Connections can include professionals in finance, real estate, business mentors, and peers who motivate you.

2. **Mentorship:**
   - Having mentors can accelerate your growth by giving insights, resources, and advice that may not be easily accessible elsewhere.

3. **Partnerships and Alliances:**
   - Building partnerships can lead to valuable collaborations and ventures, especially when entering new markets or industries.

Actionable Steps:

1. **Attend Events and Workshops:**
   - Conferences, seminars, and local meetups help connect with professionals and mentors in relevant fields.

2. **Join Online Communities:**
   - LinkedIn groups, financial forums, and industry-specific platforms provide networking opportunities virtually.

3. **Invest in Relationships:**
    - Building lasting relationships requires consistent communication and genuine interest in others' success.
4. **Seek Mentorship Programs:**
    - Many organizations and associations offer structured mentorship opportunities.
5. **Leverage Referrals:**
    - Ask existing connections to introduce you to other professionals, expanding your network further

Chapter 14: Creating Multiple Income Streams

Diversifying income sources is essential for financial security and building wealth. Relying on a single income stream can be risky, especially in uncertain economic times. Multiple streams create stability and provide a way to grow wealth consistently.

Key Concepts:

1. **Active vs. Passive Income:**
   - Active income requires ongoing effort, like a job, whereas passive income generates revenue over time with minimal maintenance, such as investments or royalties.
2. **Investment Opportunities:**
   - Stocks, bonds, real estate, and other investments offer opportunities to earn passive income and grow wealth.
3. **Entrepreneurial Ventures:**
   - Building businesses or side hustles can provide an additional income source and long-term potential for financial growth.
4. **Real Estate Investment:**
   - Owning rental properties, flipping houses, or investing in real estate funds can yield steady passive income.

Actionable Steps:

1. **Assess Income Options:**
   - Identify viable income streams that match your interests, skills, and resources.

2. **Research Investments:**
   - Look into low-cost options like ETFs, mutual funds, or even micro-investing apps to start building passive income.
3. **Start a Side Hustle:**
   - Consider skills or hobbies you can monetize, whether it's consulting, freelancing, or e-commerce.
5. **Invest in Real Estate:**
   - Explore options like rental properties, REITs, or real estate crowdfunding if direct ownership isn't feasible.
6. **Automate Savings for Investments:**
   - Dedicate a portion of your monthly earnings towards investment accounts to grow wealth steadily.

Chapter 15: Leveraging Your Credit as a Financial Tool

Credit, when managed responsibly, can be a powerful asset in building wealth and funding your dreams. Understanding how to use credit strategically will help you achieve your goals without falling into debt traps.

Key Concepts:

1. **Building a Strong Credit Score:**
   - Your credit score impacts everything from loan interest rates to potential job opportunities. Building and maintaining a good score is crucial.
2. **Responsible Use of Credit Cards:**
   - Avoid carrying a balance, pay on time, and understand the benefits of rewards programs without overspending.
3. **Leveraging Good Credit for Investment:**
   - With a solid credit score, you can access lower rates on loans, giving you more flexibility to invest in assets like real estate or businesses.
4. **Credit as a Safety Net:**
   - When used responsibly, credit can act as a backup during emergencies, preventing the need to liquidate investments.

Actionable Steps:

1. **Check Your Credit Report:**
   - Regularly review your credit report to correct errors and understand factors affecting your score.

2. **Build Credit with Secured Cards if Necessary:**
   - If you're new to credit, secured cards can help establish your credit history without high risk.
3. **Avoid Maxing Out Cards:**
   - Aim to keep credit utilization below 30% of your available limit to improve your credit score.
4. **Use Credit for Asset-Building Purchases Only:**
   - Borrow strategically, focusing on assets that will appreciate or generate income, like property.
5. **Maintain a Debt Repayment Plan:**
   - If you carry a balance, create a realistic plan to pay it down while continuing to grow your credit score.

Chapter 16: Building Your Personal Financial Network

Building a network that can support your economic growth is about connecting with people and resources that align with your goals. A robust financial network can offer you opportunities, guidance, and leverage that boost your wealth and security.

Key Concepts:
1. **Networking with Financial Professionals:**
    - Advisors, mentors, and even accountants play pivotal roles in expanding your financial strategies.
2. **Investment Partnerships:**
    - Partnering with others can open doors to investments that may be out of reach individually.
3. **Diversifying Income Sources:**
    - Diversify by exploring multiple streams, such as stocks, real estate, or business partnerships.

Actionable Steps:
1. **Join Local and Online Financial Groups:**
    - Seek out communities where you can learn and share insights on wealth building.
2. **Attend Financial Seminars and Workshops:**
    - These events often attract like-minded individuals who can become valuable contacts in your network.

3. **Collaborate with Trusted Partners:**
    - Vet potential partners carefully, aiming to work with those who share your financial goals and ethics.
4. **Invest in Personal Development:**
    - Learning about financial planning, networking, and negotiation improves your ability to navigate complex financial situations.

Chapter 17: Credit as a Tool for Empowerment

Credit, when managed wisely, can be a powerful tool for creating opportunities. By building a strong credit profile, you open doors to assets and investments that increase your wealth.

Key Concepts:

1. **Understanding Credit Scores and Reports:**
   - Your credit score affects loan approvals, interest rates, and more. Regularly review your report and understand what impacts your score.
2. **Using Credit for Investments:**
   - Strategic use of credit can enable investments in real estate, business, or education that yield returns over time.

Actionable Steps:

1. **Monitor Your Credit Regularly:**
   - Use apps or services that offer free credit monitoring to stay informed.
2. **Manage Debt Responsibly:**
   - Aim to keep your credit utilization low and pay bills on time to strengthen your score.
3. **Leverage Credit for Long-Term Assets:**
   - Use loans or credit only for investments that appreciate, like property or education, rather than consumables.

4. Build Relationships with Lenders:
  • Positive relationships with banks or financial institutions can provide you better credit terms over time.

Chapter 18: Creating and Growing a Financial Network

A well-developed financial network provides support, resources, and access to new opportunities. Cultivating connections with industry experts, peers, and mentors can be transformative for personal and business growth.

Key Concepts:

1. **Building Strategic Relationships:**
   - Networking with professionals in your field or investment sector allows you to learn, collaborate, and grow.
2. **Access to Resources and Knowledge:**
   - A strong network provides diverse insights and often leads to new opportunities and partnerships.

Actionable Steps:

1. **Attend Industry Events and Seminars:**
   - Regularly attend networking events to meet potential mentors and partners.
2. **Engage on Professional Platforms:**
   - Use platforms like LinkedIn to connect with and learn from professionals who align with your goals.
3. **Seek Mentorship:**
   - A mentor offers guidance and helps you avoid costly mistakes. Build relationships with those who have experience in areas you aspire to grow in.

Chapter 19: Business Growth on a Global Scale

This chapter explores strategies to expand your business reach globally, identifying new markets and fostering international relationships for sustained growth.

Key Concepts:

1. **Identifying Global Opportunities:**
    *   Research and analyze emerging markets that align with your product or service.
2. **Navigating Cultural Differences:**
    *   Understand and respect cultural distinctions to build trust and connections in international markets.

Actionable Steps:

1. **Develop a Global Business Plan:**
    *   Set clear goals, understand international regulations, and identify target regions for expansion.
2. **Establish Local Partnerships:**
    *   Collaborate with local businesses to ease entry into new markets and benefit from local expertise.
3. **Utilize Digital Marketing Tools:**
    *   Leverage social media and global platforms to reach international audiences.

Conclusion

As we close the first volume of The TSO Self-Empowerment Secrets Exposed, I hope you feel a renewed sense of possibility and the potential for transformation in your life. We've journeyed together through foundational steps that foster resilience, inspire growth, and ignite the drive to overcome limitations. This is the beginning—a critical starting point for breaking free from past constraints and building the mindset, habits, and purpose that form the basis of true self-empowerment.

In Volume 2, we'll dive deeper into the specifics of financial growth, with a particular focus on building and leveraging personal credit. Personal credit is a cornerstone of economic empowerment, and understanding it in detail will give you the tools to expand your financial options and strategically lay the groundwork for future endeavors. I'll guide you through actionable strategies and provide insight into credit-building techniques designed to help you establish a reliable financial network, positioning you for even greater success.

For those ready to accelerate their journey, TSO Enterprises Inc. offers personal consultations to provide you with tailored advice and support as you begin implementing these principles. By working with us, you'll gain access to resources and expert guidance to ensure you're equipped for each step in this transformative process. Together, we can develop a strategic, customized path that aligns with your unique goals.

Remember, empowerment is a journey, not a destination. Let this be the moment you take control, and know that Volume 2 will be waiting when you're ready to deepen your financial understanding and take the next step in building a prosperous future.

Sincerely,
Ronald Roscoe
Founder & Chairman, TSO Enterprises Inc
Website: www.tsoinc.us
Email: self@tsoinc.us
Phone: 877-763-7227

Made in the USA
Columbia, SC
07 December 2024